THE WITNESSES

The Witnesses

CLIVE SANSOM

METHUEN & CO. LTD
11 New Fetter Lane, London E.C.4

First published 1956
as 'The Witnesses and other Poems'
This edition first published 1971
SBN 416 08360 9

Printed in Great Britain by Fletcher & Son Ltd, Norwich

ACKNOWLEDGMENTS

The Witnesses was one of three long poems selected by the Arts Council of Great Britain for the Festival of Britain, and was printed in *Poems 1951*. I am grateful to the Arts Council and to Penguin Books Ltd, for permission to reprint.

A recording of *The Witnesses* has been issued by the. Argo Record Company.

C.S.

ACKNOWLEDGMENTS

CONTENTS

THE WITNESSES

A Composite Portrait

Mary of Nazareth—I

IT was like music:
  Hovering and floating there
With the sound of lutes and tymbrels
In the night air.

It was like waves,
Beating upon the shore:
Insistent with a rhythm, a pulsing
Unfelt before.

It was like wind:
Blowing from off the seas
Of other, far other
Lands than these.

It was like wings,
Like whirring wings that fly—
The song of an army of swans
On the dark sky.

It was like God:
A presence of blinding light,
Ravishing body and soul
In the Spring night.

The Innkeeper's Wife

I LOVE this byre. Shadows are kindly here.
 The light is flecked with travelling stars of dust.
So quiet it seems after the inn-clamour,
Scraping of fiddles and the stamping feet.
Only the cows, each in her patient box,
Turn their slow eyes, as we and the sunlight enter,
Their slowly rhythmic mouths.

                            'That is the stall,
Carpenter. You see it's too far gone
For patching or repatching. My husband made it,
And he's been gone these dozen years and more . . .'
Strange how this lifeless thing, degraded wood
Split from the tree and nailed and crucified
To make a wall, outlives the mastering hand
That struck it down, the warm firm hand
That touched my body with its wandering love.
'No, let the fire take them. Strip every board
And make a new beginning. Too many memories lurk
Like worms in this old wood. That piece you're holding—
That patch of grain with the giant's thumbprint—
I stared at it a full hour when he died:
Its grooves are down my mind. And that board there
Baring its knot-hole like a missing jig-saw—
I remember another hand along its rim.
No, not my husband's, and why I should remember
I cannot say. It was a night in winter.
Our house was full, tight-packed as salted herrings—
So full, they said, we had to hold our breaths
To close the door and shut the night-air out!
And then two travellers came. They stood outside
Across the threshold, half in the ring of light
And half beyond it. I would have let them in
Despite the crowding—the woman was past her time—
But I'd no mind to argue with my husband,

2

The flagon in my hand and half the inn
Still clamouring for wine. But when trade slackened,
And all our guests had sung themselves to bed
Or told the floor their troubles, I came out here
Where he had lodged them. The man was standing
As you are now, his hand smoothing that board.—
He was a carpenter, I heard them say.
She rested on the straw, and on her arm
A child was lying. None of your creased-faced brats
Squalling their lungs out. Just lying there
As calm as a new-dropped calf—his eyes wide open,
And gazing round as if the world he saw
In the chaff-strewn light of the stable lantern
Was something beautiful and new and strange.
Ah well, he'll have learnt different now, I reckon,
Wherever he is. And why I should recall
A scene like that, when times I would remember
Have passed beyond reliving, I cannot think.
It's a trick you're served by old possessions:
They have their memories too—too many memories.
Well, I must go in. There are meals to serve.
Join us there, Carpenter, when you've had enough
Of cattle-company. The world is a sad place,
But wine and music blunt the truth of it.'

A Shepherd in Nazareth

MORNINGS I like best,
    When, after the paling of the sky
And slow star-trembling,
The sun comes up behind Decapolis
Flooding the hills with gold.
Slowly, a prophet's vision,
The plain of Esdraelon
Smooths like a lake towards Samaria.

Then I remember tales
Of how the Canaanites were slaughtered there,
How chariots of Babylon and Egypt
Clashed on its surface once—
Now calm as sheepland,
No enemy but the fox.
Round it circle the hills,
Grazing on fields of mist—
Hump after hump
Pierced like a shield by closer cypresses—
Hills that knew Saul and Naboth,
Where Elijah walked, and priests of Baal
Drew fire from heaven.
All is quiet now. Only
Some cock's clarion down in Nazareth,
A dog disputing with the dawn,
An early wind
Combing the grass-scalp.
The sun mounts higher. Below,
Orchards of figs appear, and olive groves,
And limestone walls of houses.
The first lark rises from the tasselled grass,
Singing its way to heaven.

Out of the moving mists
A boy comes,
Tunic blue to the knee, girdled and sandalled,
Walking as if a part
Of the wind and morning.
Often he comes this way,
Lost in his thoughts and the flowers round him,
Sometimes stooping
By lily and anemone,
Peering into its cup as a child does,
Finding a world there.
Once I saw him kneel,
Head bent to the grasses,

4

And when he rose and passed me here
At twenty paces,
Thoughtful, unseeing,
His hands were a-flutter round a bird,
A sparrow fallen.
There he goes now
Down the steep hillside,
Gazing towards Galilee,
Till the waving grass and the sheep hide him.
The sun's warmth grows like a fire—
The final shiver of night.
Far down, at the corn's edge,
The first reapers
Swinging like the wind.

Joseph

HE is a good lad—never given us any trouble:
Knows how to use plane and chisel,
The different feels of wood.
Since he could grasp a nail he's helped me here,
Held planks for measuring,
And watched while I fashioned yokes and ploughs.
He'll be a craftsman—he has the hands . . .

Just twelve. Next March he'll come with us
Up to Jerusalem for the Passover.
A man already—and only yesterday
I built the cradle for him. Yes, time passes.
He knows his books, the Rabbi says,
Better than he does—that's his joke, of course—
And cuts his letters in the sand
As clear as any scholar.
Friday's trumpet never bothers him,
And Sabbaths he marches to the House of Gathering

5

Like other boys to sport. You should see him
Sitting cross-legged among the scattered herbs
Watching the readers' mouths, to taste
The flavour of their words!
Then the Prophets: quite often he is chosen—
Mary's proud then—and reads their thoughts as his.
A ringing voice. Isaiah's his favourite.

Now? Out on the hills, if I know him,
Keeping the larks company. You will see.
He'll be in to breakfast with the dream on him,
But cheerful and ready for work. . . .
Here he comes now! (See how his eyes go first
To the sacred scroll nailed to the doorpost.)
Good morning, lad! A friend to see us—
Eli from Capernaum passing through
To Caesarea. Your mother's bracelet—
That was his, and excellent workmanship.

That timber? It came last night. . . .
Well, you must learn it some time:
Crosses. At least the cross-beams for them.
We have to make them. . . . Judas the Galilean
And all his followers.
The young fool, Eli. He raised a rebellion
Against the census—you'll have heard of it—
'No King but God' their cry. Ten thousand of them,
And only two survive.
Yes, they stormed the armoury at Tiberias,
Seizing its weapons; but they stood no chance
Against the Romans. General Varus broke them
Like a dead branch, then burnt Sepphoris—
We saw the flames from here—
Till morning, not a house, not a single house;
Women and children shipped to slavery,
And those remaining from the massacre
Now to be crucified. Yes, every one.

A hideous death.
I'd sooner lose the money twenty times
Than be a party to it. But Roman orders:
'All carpenters within ten miles.'
Poor luckless fellows! Why did they do it?
Why can't they understand that violence
Only breeds violence?—that those who take the sword
Will perish by the sword? I know, I know,
But there are other ways to right men's wrongs
Than washing them in blood. God did not set us
Here on this little world to kill each other,
I'm sure of that. He loves his children
As I love Jesus here. We cannot serve him
By actions he abhors. Only by pursuing
The work he made for us—farming or carpentry
Or what you will—by loving God
And loving God in man. . . . Coming, Mary!
The other room, Eli: the meal is ready
And I've talked long enough. Come, lad. Come.
We'll pray for them—yes, and for all mankind
Wandering so far from God.

A Villager

'My father says . . .' What does your father say?
That the Messiah will change men's hearts
And snatch them whole to heaven?
What good is that?
What good is glory in the sky
With neither wine nor marriage
Nor power to taste them, tell me that?
He says . . . I know he says.
By what authority? Doors and windowframes
Are Joseph's line, not holy prophecies. . . .
Not only in heaven, boy!

When the Messiah comes in all his glory
With clouds for cushions,
He'll snuff the stars like rushlights,
Prick out the bladdered moon, and pin the sun
High in a blazing sky till doomsday morning!
You don't believe it? Listen.
When the Christ comes, says Rabbi Eleazar,
Our figs will swell to melons;
Each grain of wheat big as an ox's kidney;
And as for grapes, I tell you,
One grape—a wagonload!—
We'll tap it like a cask and float to Paradise
Here in our own backyard.
Don't talk of heaven, boy!

The Rabbi in the Temple

HIDDEN at first by heads and shoulders,
    His face suddenly confronted me,
As faces will in a congregation—
Fine head, eyes luminous and tranquil,
Expression earnest, world-forgetting,
As only youth's can be.
How long he had been squatting there
Is hard to say. Pilgrims were round him
From half the world. I tried to place them
By clothing and odd tricks of speech,
Whether from Beersheba or Damascus,
From Persia, from the banks of Tigris
Or Euphrates. . . . Then, as I say,
I noticed him. He was listening
With unfrowning keenness to the questions
Part boy, part man. They were the usual
Advanced each year upon the Terrace—
David's descendants—Patriotism—

8

When would the Anointed come?
I answered them as best I could,
Suiting reply to questioner.
Gradually, as one will sometimes
Marking a sympathetic face,
I found myself addressing him
And had deliberately to avoid
The lad, lest others, following my glance,
Should cause him such embarrassment
As again only youth can suffer.
But as the Temple's shadows fell
Across the Kedron, and the walls
Darkened, and the Roman guard
Was changed on the Tower of Antony;
When the swifts rose higher, screaming,
And the last remnants of the crowd
Dispersed; I called him over.

His parents had set out that morning
Towards Nazareth. He'd left the city,
With other children from that village
Around the tail-end of the caravan;
But on the road, near Gethsemane,
He recalled this Terrace-questioning
As seen from the Court of Gentiles,
And something in him—some instinct
Stronger than reason or family ties,
The hunger of an expanding mind—
Plucked him away from them,
Compelled him to return.
He had eaten nothing. With a message,
I sent him to my sister's husband,
His house by the Street of Tailors,
Where he supped and slept.
Next morning, he appeared again
Under the cedared roof, but having,
As I suppose, lost awe of me,

He put some questions too—more simple
Than profound: Why death must be?
Why pain and love should co-exist?
God's plan for Israel—but with so keen
A purpose, such unsensual passion,
As if his spirit would uncover
The very nucleus of truth
Though it destroy him, that my heart
Melted and I loved the boy.

That night I talked of him to Hillel
And other doctors, and the third morning,
Most of the pilgrims having left,
They joined my group, and struck as I was
By the lad's marked sincerity,
Spoke to him freely and he to them
Till humble query and learned answer
Flowered to discussion among equals.
And then . . . and then his mother came,
Foolish like all mothers, with cries
Of 'Where'd he been?', 'Why treat them so?'
He—poised between serenity
And anger, seeing her standing there
Distressed, relieved, the husband
Embarrassed under the arch behind—
Surrendered to her. 'Where should I be,'
He asked, 'but in my Father's house?'
The significance, I think, was lost,
For she looked puzzled, turned to her husband,
And thought of home. She took his arm,
Physical contact being necessary
When a spiritual bond is lost,
And with an apology to us—
For his delightful talking, mark you,
Not for her interruption!—drew him
Down to the lower courtyard. At the stairs
He turned. His face held mine an instant.

The sunlight caught his hair. The high council
Was over, he a boy again.

That must be twenty years ago.
Often since then, Passover-time,
I've asked myself, 'Who was the lad,
And what's become of him?'
God's not so lavish with such faces
He moulds them to no purpose . . .
What's that noise? Why are they shouting
Down in the outer court? What's that?
Some firebrand causing trouble,
Denouncing sellers and exchangers,
Upsetting tables? Incredible!
Young men to-day, they have no—
No respect, no decency.
'Soiling my Father's house with trade'
Impertinence! *His father's house!*

Where have I heard that phrase?

The Brothers

GOING from Nazareth? Where?—To the Jordan valley?
Leaving your home and your trade, your own kinsfolk?
For what? For an unwashed preacher, a ranting hermit
Who sacrificed family and wealth, and a seat in the priesthood
For locusts and prophecies? Why—you are mad, insane,
Selling your life for a whim, a religious frenzy.
Mad, yes, mad. Will you share his faith and his filth,
Outcast like him, rejected by brother and friend,
A life of rebellion, hunger, a shameful death?

If the thought of that leaves you unmoved, then remember us
Your brothers and sisters; the mother who gave you birth.

See her there, standing in tears, forsaken, bewildered,
Left by her first-born, you, the head of the household.
Think of her neighbours' looks, the humiliation,
Her fears and her griefs. What? What do you say?
'Whoever obeys the will of my father in heaven
Is my brother, my sister, my mother.'—By the God of Israel!
Would you preach at us?—your ministry start at home?
Better recall, if you can, your father in Nazareth,
Your pledge to him, your promise of filial care.
'You shall honour your father and mother,'—Remember that
When you mouth your texts. Remember that:
And carry for ever the shame of your father's children.

John, the Baptist

CRIER, not prophet was I sent—
    The voice of one
Proclaiming in the wilderness, 'Have done!
Repent! Repent!'

Scorched rock and stunted thorn my home,
Jackal my friend,
Hewing a path to God, that in the end
God's son may come.

Follow no Christ, hail no Messiah
Till he arise.
Only with living water I baptize:
He with fire!

Come to this ford on the Jordan river,
Come down and wait.
Cleanse your hearts; drown in the waters' spate
Your wrongs for ever.

Farmers, craftsmen—and you who stand,
Young fishers yonder,
Watching from river-reed and oleander—
The hour's at hand.

You, priests' spies—who turn theology
Into a tidy sum—
Expect no shelter from the wrath to come,
Sadducee! Pharisee!

You shall not—no, do what you can—
Delay that hour,
Nor bribe, with your legalities and power,
The Son of Man.

Stop! Look!—under the tamarisk tree—
See!—there he stands!
Those Devil-mastering eyes, God-serving hands . . .
It is He—He!

Andrew

IT was like this: near to Gennesaret
Where the hot springs pour their streams into the lake,
And the fish gather like little Romans
To loll in its warmth, though at a hint of danger,
Swift as kingfishers in the air above,
Flash from the shallows—there one evening
When the sun, sinking behind Tiberias,
Brought the far shore closer,
And the water lay calm, unrippled,
And no wind blew. . . .
It was then, with his own peace, he came.

Simon and I were casting together,
Thigh-deep in the liquid sunset.
Herod's barge had passed in the distance.
Whirling my weighted net about my head
I watched it fall, open and spread
Like the skirts of a dancer.
As it sank to the lake-floor
I pulled the cord and, the mouth closing,
Was dragging it beachward. . . . There he stood—
Smiling seriously at our surprise—
Jesus—last seen with the Baptist.
Our dropped nets bulged on the pebbles.
'Come with me. . . . You will fish for men.'

The wild fish, silvered, sunlit,
Leapt and writhed in the loose netting.

The Woman of Samaria

HE came to me with his eyes and asked for water,
    Stretched out his hands and spoke.
His mind burned into mine like the noon sun,
My pitcher of thoughts broke.

I had not noticed him at rest by the well-head,
Shadowed by the rare tree;
But as I carried my shame into its coolness
His eyes awaited me.

I tried to avoid them as I drew the well-rope
Taut through a mindless hand.
I saw his robe cross the speckled sunlight,
His feet stir the hot sand.

14

I saw his face. It was white with road-dust,
Whiter than any stone.
But his eyes were ageless and deep as well-shafts
As they met my own.

They unroofed my brain with their profound gazing,
Made the heart a molten thing:
Every purdahed thought unveiled itself
Under their questioning.

He spoke of water to cleanse the spirit:
I tried not to understand.
He followed me along the road of my evasions,
And when it ceased in sand

He brought me home from my self-forced journey—
He showed me my own soul
Cracked and dry as a discarded wine-skin,
And made it whole. . . .

He came to me with his eyes and asked for water,
Stretched out his hands and spoke.
As I carried my peace back to the streets of Sychar,
A new world woke.

Nicodemus

YOU will say I am ancient and cautious as a tortoise:
    Yes, and you would be right. But can he help
Being a tortoise? And can I help being I?
Is it possible to cast one's nature like a snakeskin
By desire and will, by an act of the imagination?
He said men could, and I once believed him,
Though, in my character, only cautiously believed.
Custom, I suppose, dictates: a sheltered childhood,

Comfort and servants; every move prescribed,
Every request forestalled. And later, in scholarship,
Walking along the carefully-trodden paths,
Fitting my sandals in the approved footprints.
To others, no doubt, an object of admiration,
But to me, who lived closer to myself than they did,
Lacking one last possession, I lacked all.
For you see: though I could quote the Scriptures,
Arguing for hours on the minutest quibble,
My philosophy was valueless. I could discuss life,
But life itself, the final mystery,
Always eluded me. What was its purpose?
Could man, incomplete, complete himself?
Unsatisfied, find satisfaction?

Then one day—it was Passover time—
Hearing tales of this travelling preacher,
I dared my orthodoxy to the point of listening.
He was a young man, barely thirty,
Formerly a carpenter, they said, from the north country,
Though with his plain tunic and plainer speech
It was hard to place him. Instantly I knew—
Young as he was, old and confirmed as I—
He held some knowledge, some instinctive truth,
That one who read himself blind on occasions
Never possessed: the very core of life.
Impossible for me, a member of the Sanhedrin,
Intellectually omnipotent, to address him there—
The respectable tortoise must respect his shell!
But I spoke to a disciple—John, I think—
And arranged a meeting later in his lodgings.
It was a clear night—the Passover moon,
And a strong wind blowing. Concealing myself
Under my cloak, drawing it around my face—
A precaution against the wind, I assured myself—
I followed him down a labyrinth of streets
Till I found myself standing by an upper window

In full moonlight, high above the city,
The white light burnished on the temple roof.
'It is he, master—Nicodemus. . . .'
I saw him watch my wrinkled neck emerge,
And knew he knew me. 'You,' I began,
Hiding beneath words, 'Are a teacher sent from God.'
It was difficult to continue, wanting knowledge
And afraid of knowledge. He read my silence.
'No man can reach the Kingdom by thought alone:
He must be re-born in the spirit.'
He spoke to a part of me I had often silenced,
Fearing the consequences of its rashness.
I sought my shell again, feigning stupidity.
'How, master, can a man have two births?'
He: 'Unless the spirit conceives in him,
The Kingdom will never come.'
Another silence. Only the cool night wind
Rustling my silken robe, stirring the trees.
I feared the fierceness of his truth might break me,
Like a thrush with a snail. The more I believed,
The stronger I must deny. 'How is it possible?
How can God's spirit enter us and renew?'
He quietly: 'No need to question how
It happens: the happening is enough.
The wind blows where it will. You hear the sound
And know its presence. But who can say
Where it has come from, where it goes?'
Silence again. Someone preparing beds.
Outside, the trees like a distant sea,
Like waves breaking. What chance had half an hour
With half a century of custom and observance?
Sadly I left him there and came away
Covering my ears—symbolic act—
Never to meet again.

But still I had news of him, followed him in my mind
(Least arduous of journeys) up into Galilee,

Up through the fertile valleys of Samaria
Into the lake country and the Phoenician hills,
Desiring his living presence more than life,
Yet dreading more than death its consequence.
Then in the third year, again at Passover,
He approached Jerusalem. I prayed that he might retreat,
For his sake as for mine. The Sanhedrin met,
Debating how to kill him—face after face
Passionate for his end. I did not mean to speak.
No: not courage. I had no thought of speaking.
My heart beat so loudly on the bench behind,
I rose to silence it. 'Our law
(Gripping the rail in front) condemns
No man without a hearing . . .' I sank back
Trembling and exhausted, my spirit sapped
More than by hours of argument. The faces
Were turned to mine. 'Are you from Galilee?'
'Has he bedevilled you as well?'—amazed
(No more than I) at my temerity.
Noting the grey flagstone between my feet,
I left their taunts unanswered. My power had gone.
When he was arraigned before the Council,
I pleaded sickness, kept to my house
And drew my head in. With shame and sadness
I learned the sentence—unjust, unlawful.
Crucified by indecision, the two-way mind,
Torn as a body is between wild horses,
I uttered nothing, protested nothing,
Listening to the duologue of my opposing selves.
And then, by evening, when it was all over,
I, too, was dead. Dead to all feeling,
A breathing corpse, a walking conscience,
I came into the air. In the Bazaar of Spices
I purchased myrrh and aloes—enough
To serve the burial of an Egyptian king.
It impressed the merchant. Me, Nicodemus,
It did not impress. With easy gold

I paid for the Christ's embalming; but to him,
The living Christ, I had offered nothing—
Less than a child's look or a passing cheer.
I try to forget—routine's a great embalmer—
Follow the pattern of my tapering days
Towards another tomb. Sometimes I succeed.
Sometimes I convince myself that prudence
Is man's greatest virtue, tortoisehood
His supreme achievement.
Only, some evenings, when the night wind blows,
My spirit stirs again, and I remember.

Matthew

To others he was a presence—perhaps only
A glance, an arrested gesture. But to me
A voice always, always a voice. When I think of him
It is words that I remember. No, more than that,
The tone behind the words, the emphasis
Driving them home in argument, nailing them
Beyond the reach of scribes; the inflexion
That dealt their thought directly to the heart;
Or the rhythm bearing them like a stream
Through fields of parable. Yes, and behind all these
—Calm or impassioned, Hebrew or Aramaic—
That constant quality, the essential He.

Capernaum! It was in that microcosm,
That inn for the lake-trade—vivid confusion
Of men and reflexions toiling together, and anchorage
For the landfleet caravans. The smell of fish
And heavy cloth-dyes, the smoke from the tile kilns;
But above all else in that kaleidoscope:
Noise—the torrent, avalanche of sound.
The hot shell of my toll-booth hid the rest—

Image and colour—all but smells and sounds. . . .
The market-hum—in half a dozen tongues,
Greek, Roman, Jewish, Arab—smoothed by distance
Into a common dialect. . . . Nearer,
The cries of gulls, disputing, bargaining. . . .
Orders shouted from the quay, the crash of fish-crates.

Silence. Or so it seemed. The sounds
Faded. Only, plaintive, high up,
The gulls, and round the coins on my desk
The flies buzzing.
And then a voice, his voice,
Unhurried, vibrant:
'Follow me.'
Two words. They were enough.
I followed him.

The Madman of Gergesa

FELLOW self within my self,
  Follows and torments myself—
Hear, behind this wordy night,
Wind-grunts and the snorts of night,
Voices stumbling up the cliff,
Repeating, beating on the cliff,
Matching echo in my brain,
The endless echo of my brain.
When we left Tiberias,
Finger-eyed Tiberias,
You we two sought safety here,
Thought we could find safety here
In this rockhill caved with tombs—
Only dumb men house in tombs.
Lied, you lied! See, stumbling near us,
(Cliff-torn child-rocks crumbling near us)

Man there in the lamp of moon,
Dead man risen in the moon.
What have I to do with you,
Jesus, what to do with you?
Keep your words! torment me not!
Son of God, torment me not!
Name—he questions for our name.
Tell him nothing. Name no name
Lest his powers untenant us:
Mangod will untenant us.
Listen! sh! he talks to me—
No-one between him and me.
Try to hear and not to hear:
Self-in-self may overhear.
Words, the voice that stunned the storm,
Still might still this other storm.
Once he knows that I am many,
If he only knows how many
Ghosts of self inhabit self,
He will banish self from self,
Drown it deeper than the lake,
Deeper down than deepest lake.
Voice—that voice is my religion—
Lord! Christ! Friend!—my name is legion!

Mary of Magdala

BRUISED were my breasts with the weight of men,
    Uncounted men,
Unknown before and in an hour
    Unknown again:

Bruised my brain by each loveless love,
        Each casual thrust;
My spirit lying corrupted, foul,
        In its tomb of lust.

He found me, raised me like Lazarus
 From that living grave,
Showed me I still had a self to honour,
 A soul to save.

I wiped my lips and bound my hair,
 And to men's surprise
No longer walked through the Street of Doves
 With sidelong eyes.

I was a woman once more—delivered
 From a second birth,
Possessed by none but God and he
 In the whole earth.

Oh, oil and tears were little to pay—
 Nor a heart riven—
For the wealth of his love, his giving love,
 And the grace of heaven.

The Phoenician Woman

'SHE has followed us all day, master, hooknosed, insistent,
 Yapping at our heels in commercial Greek:
Her husband a boat-builder—those boats of gopher-wood,
Her daughter, it seems, possessed of a devil
Which you, master, a Jew, are supposed to exorcize.
Talk to her, master, send her away.
Tell her you came to the children of Israel,
Not to Phoenician dogs.'

He turned on me sternly. But his voice smiled.
'You hear what they say?' he demanded.
'Is it right, do you think, taking the children's food
And tossing it to the dogs?'

'Master,' I replied, feeling the bond between us,
A humour we shared alone,
'Even dogs are allowed scraps from the table
When the children reject them.'
His face smiled too.
'You have understanding and faith, mother:
It will happen as you desire.'

It was true. Coming to the hill above Tyre,
Weary beyond all weariness, I fell on my knees,
Letting my eyes search where feet could not follow.
Looking down on the cluster of evening ships,
The causeway with its moving chain of carriers
And the heap of murex-shells outside the dye-works,
I saw her coming from the bazaars to meet me,
Her white conspicuous among blues and purples.
She did not need to speak.
She walked up the hill as a girl walks
Whose arms are her own.

Peter

FOR a while, Mark, lay your scroll aside.
    I need your eyes. When I'm dictating
I think in words. That kind of thinking
Blurs what's behind the words. You see,
I'm no scholar, friend—nor ever will be.
Words come hardly to me, very hardly.
Though I have fought them for our Master's sake,
I'll never be their master. Talking's all right:
You see the other's face; talking is natural.
But when I watch you setting down my speech
In black and white, it puts my tongue in fetters.
So this evening, Mark, just let me say
My memories to you. I want to recall

23

This clearer than the rest—it most concerns me.
I would remember and re-live
What happened on the road to Caesarea,
Those years ago.

We were walking despondently towards the city
Discouraged and alone. Driven from Galilee,
Each had his own regrets. Yes, even he
Was sorrowful—I sensed it—saying little,
Scarcely answering. . . . Then all at once
The sound of water. We raised our heads,
And, rearing over us, a cliff of limestone,
Brilliant in sunlight. Streaks of iron, like blood,
Ran down it, and from a cave
Half down the rock, the Jordan river
Descending from the heights of Hermon
Poured out its spring-clear waters. We stopped,
Seeing the city of Caesarea
Behind a lace of spray—the trees,
White roofs and towers. It should have lifted us,
That sudden vision. Somehow it didn't.
It made us more despondent. For I thought—
Or was it he who thought and I who felt him?—
This water that is born so hopefully
Ends in the Dead Sea's useless desolation.
Abruptly he asked, 'Who do men say I am?'
We answered variously, 'John the Baptist, risen',
'Elijah or Jeremiah', 'One of the prophets'.
Silence, the water speaking. Then he asked:
'Who do *you* say I am?' Another silence—
Only a moment, but enough to tell
Our disillusionment. I cried—
No, rather I heard the words drawn from me—
The voice was not my own: 'You are the Christ,
Son of the living God!' He turned to me
Transfigured. His face was God's.
'Peter' (he named me then), 'You are the rock

On which I build my church. The gates of hell
Shall not prevail against you.' Oh, Mark,
Men have their moments.—That was mine,
The phrase I'd lived for. Since then
I have betrayed it—doubted, denied,
Deserted him. But always
Those words return, with their background
Of falling water, each time
More powerful than before. For he saw me,
Not as I was, but as I might become.
His faith has hardened me. In course of time
The rock has petrified. When that hour comes
When I must follow him who questioned me,
I shall not fail again. The gates of hell,
As he once prophesied, shall not prevail.

The Youth at the Pool of Siloam

MY world was night
      Until he came.
The sun's light
      And the fire's flame

Warmly spoke
      To this wall of skin,
Yet never woke
      The fires within.

Faces were voices,
      Moving lips,
Hollows and spaces
      For finger-tips;

But something under
Each fluttering lid
Told of the wonder
My darkness hid:

And as I lay
By the Gate and clutched
The bowl one day,
My lids were touched.

I thought, by his feeling,
That he was blind,
Those hands revealing
The touch-quick mind.

I felt my eyes,
Where his fingers lay,
Stir and rise
With the hardening clay;

And when I stooped
To wash it away,
In the water I scooped
The day was day!

The pool, it broke
Like a bowl of dye—
Unsolid, a-soak
With the autumn sky.

Sunlight talking,
Branches tossing,
The man walking,
His two legs crossing. . .

That's all my story:
Set me free.
The world is glory,
And I can see!

Martha of Bethany

It's all very well
  Sitting in the shade of the courtyard
Talking about your souls.
Someone's got to see to the cooking,
Standing at the oven all morning
With you two taking your ease.
It's all very well
Saying he'd be content
With bread and honey.
Perhaps he would—but I wouldn't,
Coming to our house like this,
Not giving him of our best.
Yes, it's all very well
Him trying to excuse you,
Saying your recipe's best,
Saying I worry too much,
That I'm always anxious.
Someone's got to worry—
And double if the others don't care.
For it's all very well
Talking of faith and belief,
But what would you do
If everyone sat in the cool
Not getting their meals?
And he can't go wandering and preaching
On an empty stomach—
He'd die in the first fortnight.
Then where would you be
With all your discussions and questions
And no one to answer them?
It's all very well.

Lazarus

Do not ask me. I cannot tell you.
   I did not wish to come.
He was my friend. I loved him.
I desired no miracle.

My soul is in that grave—or elsewhere—
Flesh-housed no longer.
I surrendered it to God, its giver,
Willed all my will to his.

I travelled past time to a region
Where the shining of planets failed—
A place of being, from whence
It is death to return.

Beautiful? I do not remember.
The bridge fell as I crossed.
I only know that that world accepted me,
And its frontiers were my own.

Reason tells me this world is lovely.
I know, but I cannot feel.
The anemones on the hillside come
No nearer than the eye.

I woke from the dark to find them—
A grinding, a wedge of light—
His beard and cheeks in the opening,
His tears that had drawn me back.

Rejoicing, they unwound the grave-clothes,
The linen strap from my chin;
But a hollow shape was revealed there—
This is my shell you see.

No messages. No questions.
I did not wish to come.
I am suspended between two meanings,
And neither word is mine.

A Child

'LET them come without hindrance:
       The Kingdom is theirs.
Be with them and of them,
In your hearts and your prayers.
For freely they enter,
Unafraid, unawares. . . .'

Like poems his talk was:
The words that he said
Were strung in the sunlight
Like pearls on a thread—
My face by his girdle,
His hand on my head.

The Rich Young Ruler

'WHAT must I do, master, to gain
       Eternal life?
From my youth I have kept the Commandments,
Honoured my parents;
Theft, murder, lying, adultery—
All these
By God's mercy have passed me by.
What then must I do, master?
What more must I do?'

'Sell all,' he replied, 'And follow me.'
An easy saying.
He, a carpenter, a carpenter's son,
Sacrificed nothing.
And his man Peter—smirking, self-righteous—
What did he lose
But some worn nets, a boat-share,
And trade in the market?
It wasn't myself I was thinking of—
Ease and possessions—
But the responsibility of wealth
Towards its dependents.
What of them, if I had obeyed him—
What of my servants?

That's what I tell myself, now—
But do I believe it?
Then—silent—I walked away,
Watching my sandals,
While his voice, the voice of my heart,
Followed me homeward.
In misery, I stopped by the lake.
Hid by the crowd-wall,
I heard him speak of the Kingdom of God,
The camel, the needle.

Zacchaeus of Jericho

I AM an old man. Eighty summers
Have creased my skin to crinkled leather.
The harsh face of the desert yonder
Has stretched between those bony rockhills,
Cracked and barren, jaundice-coloured,
Reeking of desolation.
But here the full cheeks of the city

Have flushed each year with fruit and blossom.
Dates, figs, melons and oranges
Have flourished here, and groves of balsam.
I should know, for half my summers
I took the tax on them. Abundance.
You'll find much to see. That palace
Behind the cypress: Herod built it
From Syrian marble, and in winter
Favoured us with his sciatica.
A good place for such royal ailments,
Though you're too young to care—and I, well,
I'm too old. For now, all seasons,
My days are rounded by this garden.
I sit here, in the lively shadows
Flung by this sycamore, forgetting
Far more than I remember, dreaming,
Letting the remnants of existence
Slip through its dying fingers. Only
This one thought stays with me—that once, yes,
Once when this tree and I were younger
I climbed along its leaf-thick branches,
Above the heads that filled the orchard,
To see a prophet pass. . . . Smiling?
They always do. The distant antic
And present self seem strangely wedded.
Even at the time it caused some laughter,
Seeing that little grave official
Whose days were packed with self-importance
Assume the schoolboy. What possessed me
I can't imagine. Something told me
I had to see him. And certainly
That moment changed my world. I knew then
Living was more than tithes and taxes
And rates of interest. This city
Of oils and fruits, whose lavish bounty
I'd sifted out in drams and drachmas,
Was richer than the gold that bought it;

And life intended to be lived. . .
Ah yes, good-bye. I won't detain you.
You have your business here—as I had.
Now I'm content with merging shadows,
And that exchange of past and future
We call the present. When you're returning
To Ashkelon, or on the trade-routes
To Asia, bartering peace for pay
At the earth's edge, I'll still be sitting
Here, by this sycamore, remembering.

The Donkey's Owner

SNAFFLED my donkey, he did—good luck to him!—
Rode him astride, feet dangling, near scraping the ground.
Gave me the laugh of my life when I first see them,
Remembering yesterday—you know, how Pilate come
Bouncing the same road, only that horse of his
Big as a bloody house and the armour shining
And half Rome trotting behind. Tight-mouthed he was,
Looking he owned the world.
                                        Then to-day,
Him and my little donkey! Ha!—laugh?—
I thought I'd kill myself when he first started.
So did the rest of them. Gave him a cheer
Like he was Caesar himself, only more hearty:
Tore off some palm-twigs and followed shouting,
Whacking the donkey's behind. . . . Then suddenly
We see his face.
The smile had gone, and somehow the way he sat
Was different—like he was much older—you know—
Didn't want to laugh no more.

Sadducee to Pharisee

' I T has been said. . . . But I say. . . .
   Always that formula.
Yet he denies iconoclasm,
Swearing he fulfils the law.'

'Naturally: and I agree with him—
In moderation. For where growth ends
Decay and death begin. Tradition, my friend,
Is a stream to follow,
Not a pond to sit by.'

'So you reiterate. But which stream?
Flowing in which direction? Your only guide,
It seems, is Inclination. Following him
You'll never reach the sea.'

'Oh, quite mistaken! Already
There's the whiff of salt in my nostrils.
And we move, my friend, we move.
Your company, stiff in their cerements
Of scrolls and tablets, display a corpse's
Reluctant animation.'

                'Better dead
Than damned. But all this fencing
Misses the target of our conversation
Who is threatening our beliefs, our God.'

'True, true; and worse than that,
He threatens your finances,
The temple dues, remember,
Those plump white profits
On sacrificial lambs.'

'That gibe's unworthy.
You will not, then, support
Our condemnation?'

            'On the contrary,
I will support it enthusiastically
With both hands, and witness his stoning
With the profoundest satisfaction.'

'May I ask why?'

            'Certainly—
And receive a convincing answer.
The man endangers our very existence
As a nation. Threatened with submergence
By waves of heathenism, our single hope
Lies in the observance of religious ritual,
The badge of Juda. If he continues
To profane the Sabbath, to defy the laws
Of purification, we shall disintegrate
In easy tolerance, and God's world be filled
By Hellenistic Jews and Hebraic Gentiles—
Intolerable bastardy! . . . Forgive me.
I have indulged myself in the vulgarity
Of an emotion. But appropriately
We have reached agreement and my house together.
You are heated: Come, take wine with me.'

The Dove-seller

NOT right in the head, that's my opinion—
    Striding into the temple here
As if he owned the place—calling us
'Thieves who defile my father's house'—
That's what he said, forgetting that we know

Exactly who he is and where he comes from.
Where? His home's in Nazareth, and his father
No more than you or me. Then, by God,
He turns the tables—yes, right over,
Clattering and falling like a pack of cards—
Coins spinning across the flagstones, men
Scrambling for them like hens over a cornbowl—
Squawking like hens too! Ignoring them,
He crosses to our side—we'd been sitting
Quietly selling these doves of sacrifice
Till he walks in—and calling us thieves again—
In fifteen years I've never been accused
Of overcharging—he kicks our stools away,
Starting with this one. Well, the din!
You could have heard it at the Golden Gate—
The Jaffa Gate! Then my doves got loose,
Rose to the ceiling with a whirl of wings
And settled there, while he continued
Down that long line of columns and out again
Into the sun. . . .

Caiaphas

Proceed with the utmost caution: the man is cunning.
   More than once when we've laid our nets the fish has
      escaped us,
Dissolved in a crowd of disciples, or crossed the lake
To another province, a different jurisdiction.
He knows the laws too well. He possesses a gift
Rare in these mob-stirrers, a steady intellect.
True, he may be a firebrand, a passionate denouncer,
One instant trouncing his hearers with divine love,
And soothing, the next, with imminent damnation;
But always, at the heart of that fire, there's a calm reason
Dictating whom to offend, how far to offend them.

I repeat, the fellow is cunning. He can tell at a glance
The *agent provocateur*, the subtle questioner
Setting a baited word to catch sedition:
Remember the Emperor's head and his other devices.
Deftly he releases the spring, and the trap is harmless,
Biting the free air. I counsel patience.
With all his talk of heaven and heavenly fathers,
He sees this animal world and its crawling parasites
Clearly as we do—indeed, more clearly,
For he perceives, I think, behind word and action,
The motive, concealed or disguised—that lurking stranger,
Landlord of all our thoughts. It makes him dangerous.
Therefore proceed with caution. Contempt of faith
Is no offence against Rome, and only she
Holds power over life and death. To arrest the Nazarene
Without Pilate's prior consent is to invite disaster,
And he'll ask for evidence—far stronger evidence
Than we possess at present. We need reliable witnesses
To prove subversion: these generalized reports
Are too ambiguous. And remember—once released
On charges of sedition, he'll be assumed innocent
Of blasphemy too; his flickering popularity
Take fire again, and he'll be free to go
Spreading his poisons for twenty—thirty years,
Until he dies, in bed. Let me change my metaphor.
Wait till the time is ripe. Pluck it green,
Our bowels will judge us. Suspend your appetite.
My instincts tell me. . . . Who? On urgent business?
No, I will see him now. Excuse me, gentlemen.
That season, I think, has come.
Continue your discussion. I will rejoin it
As speedily as I may.

Forgive the interruption. The moment I foresaw
Is here already. The fruit hangs ripe for picking.
One of the Nazarene's followers, a man called Judas,
Offers the evidence we desire—no enemy

Like a disappointed friend!—private conversations
Meant for their ears alone. Yes, words enough
To dam for ever the breath that spurted them.
Moreover, he says, he will lead the Temple Guard
To where they sleep at night outside the city.
This will enable us to arrest him quietly,
Without a daylight mob to cause disturbance.
Now to Pilate. He is conveniently in our debt
Regarding the appropriation of the Temple funds.
The time has come for payment—and with interest.
A moment's silence. . . . Praise to Almighty God
Who makes us instruments to-night to end these blasphemies
Against morality and truth and his holy Church.
His blessings on us all and this undertaking.

The Boy Mark

THAT night, moonbright, in the upper room,
    I served him with meat and wine.
When he told the Twelve of his coming doom
    Their grief was mine.

Unsleeping, weeping, I lay and listened
    As they talked and the hours moved on;
Till the moon rose and the white roofs glistened,
    And the last man had gone.

Then catching, snatching a sheet about me,
    Which doorways, walls concealed,
I tracked their swift shadows until they brought me
    Here to the oil-press field.

Hidden, unbidden, among silvered trees
    I tensed as he strode my way:
But a bough's length distant he dropped on his knees,
    And parted lips to pray.

These words I heard on the moonlit hill:
    'Father, hear thy son!
Remove this cup, and yet thy will,
    Not mine be done.'

Now, on his brow, great pearls of sweat
    Glisten like drops of dew.
Silently, under Olivet,
    My tears are falling too.

Three times he climbs from his lonely prayers
    To Peter, James and John,
Sighs, and returns, and leaves as theirs
    The ground they sleep upon.

Then a sound rebounds on the night air—
    A cry from the Kedron bridge.
Torches, like heartless fires, flare,
    Winding towards the ridge.

I see, through my tree, where the leaves hang dumb
    And moveless as the dead,
The dark, torch-blooded soldiers come,
    With Judas at their head.

Proud, uncowed, he keeps his tryst
    In the flarelight and the moon.
I know, too late, he is the Christ—
    Too late, or too soon.

No friend, at the end, to give him hope!
    Clutching my tangled sheet,
I fling myself wildly down the slope
    To his friendless feet. . . .

Yes, he smiled at the child—at the boy's whim—
    A smile in which love prevailed,
But I saw the men who surrounded him,
    And my courage failed

At the jeering, sneering, flickering sight,
    And here where this cypress is
I left my robe in their hands that night,
    My soul in his.

Pilate at Caesarea

FROM this deck survey the city. Nothing has changed
    Since I first came as Governor to the province.
The terraced houses shelving the waterfront,
The palaces, the great Temple of Augustus—
They all resemble the city that Spring morning
As those reflections trembling on the water. . . .
Turning, I see the ships—the same ships
That, alive with men and sunlight, anchored here
When I arrived from Alexandria—the double harbour
Broken by reefs, and the seawall Herod raised
On sunken pillars—always a tireless builder—
Circling the shipping with a protecting arm.
At the far end, its very finger-tips,
The avenue of colossi that greeted us
When, after fighting the Sicilian seas,
Our boat swept into haven—huge arms
Lifted in salutation, toga'd figures
Rotating as we swung beneath them,
And the whole harbour echoing with the cry
Procurator Caesaris!

That morning shone propitious, prophetic.
Calm waters, crowded ships, sunlight and statues,
The cheers of sailors and the waiting army
All augured a happy and successful mission.
It seems the gods deceived me. I'll not pretend
Vitellius has ordered me to Rome
To accept an Emperor's congratulations.

Men are allowed mistakes, but not too many.
I have made four too many.
Sending the ensigns into Jerusalem,
That was the first mistake. Valerius Gratus
Had counselled me to treat the Jews with firmness,
But I misjudged them. Merchants as they are,
They set the observance of religious laws
Above their lives. Swarming to Caesarea,
They colonized my courtyard on their knees,
Wailing, imploring me through palace walls—
Small sleep on either side those nights!—to remove
'The images of Caesar.' The sixth day
Insomnia and impatience conquered me.
I called a tribunal in the Hippodrome
And circled it with soldiers. At a signal,
They drew their swords. I threatened instant death
Unless they restored me my imperial peace
And found their homes again. The wrong technique.
Ripping their clothes, they bared their necks to me—
Scraggy and plump, immaculate and filthy—
Pleading decapitation to preserve
Their city's sanctity. Some might have accepted
That invitation. I was tempted to.
But they had judged me well: not amiable enough
For popularity, not ruthless enough
To enforce obedience. So, I gave way
(What else could I have done, being myself?)
Ordered the ensigns to be stationed here,
And let them go, triumphant.
                              A bad beginning.
But it taught me to ingratiate myself
With Caiaphas and his friends, the Great Sanhedrin,
Not to offend them twice. When I completed
The aqueduct—some twenty miles of it—
Bringing down water from the Artus Valley
To the rock-cisterns underneath their temple,
I preached the benefits of co-operation,

Mutual self-interest. To my astonishment
They listened, and after considerable debate
Offered towards the cost of its construction
'A voluntary contribution from the temple funds.'
My glory was short-lived. Hearing of it,
The mob began to fill the synagogues,
Cursing Procurator and priests alike;
Till memories of earlier intimidation
Drew them to my palace in Jerusalem
With cries of 'Corban!' and 'Return our money'
('Our' money, not 'our' water!) This time,
Possessing an easy conscience and the priests'
Authority, I launched a battalion
Into the tide of people, armour covered,
To crack the skulls of those who shouted loudest.
No second telling. Some of them even
Exceeded their instructions, having like me
A score to settle. Many died there,
Stretched on the flagstones. Others in panic
Trampled each other in the narrow streets
Down to the Lower City. Ten minutes
And it was over; the city quiet,
My first mistake reversed.

But errors are not consumed like forest fires
By raising others. Each miscalculation
Carries its comet's tail of consequence,
And this was no exception. Moreover,
It put a weapon in the Sanhedrin's hands
They could not fail to use. Now they would argue:
'We were persuaded to do that, remember,
Against the people's will: now you do this.'
I waited. . . . One evening
Claudia and I were sharing our first yawns
When Caiaphas was announced. She left us there.
Before he spoke, I knew his mind.
There was a prophet out of Nazareth

Collecting crowds by annotating scripture,
Curing their sores and sins—the usual claptrap.
Harmless enough, but to-day his followers
Proclaimed him King outside Jerusalem—
Dangerous for the priests, more dangerous for me.
If they arrested him before the morning,
Would I condemn? It seemed too easy.
The land was as thick with self-appointed preachers
As their shirts with lice. One prophet more or less
Would scarcely notice. Besides, the times
Were dangerous: the city full of pilgrims
Attending the feast: some carried arms; the city
Could easily be ignited. I agreed,
But paused before consenting. It was necessary
To make the act a favour of importance
Cancelling obligations. He, too, I noticed,
Successfully concealed his satisfaction.

Next morning, before the Praetorium,
The prisoner came for judgment. I saw he was
No ordinary man. There was authority
That contemplated mine and knew its weakness.
He interested me.
Instead of passing sentence, I enquired,
Using the accepted formula of a trial:
'What is your accusation against this man?'
The priests buzzed angrily. After our interview
Their witnesses were dismissed. 'He has spoken
Against taxation, against religion, declaring
He is Christ the King!' The mob snarled with them.
I turned to him for answer. None.
Yet no fear either. Within that tumult
His calm was eloquence.
I ordered him inside, into the silence,
For private interrogation. His words then
Were few enough, but he himself convinced me
The Kingdom that he preached was not Judea

Nor any other place on mortal maps—
Not mortal maps. For many minutes
I leaned against a column wondering,
Remembering Claudia's dream. Then I returned,
And said before my mind could swing again,
'I find no fault in him.' Another uproar.
I did my best to save him—sent him to Antipas,
Offered another prisoner in exchange,
Looked through each loophole in the laws. In my position
Dared I have done more? Then Caiaphas himself
Came to my shoulder. 'If you release him,
You are no friend of Caesar's.' The winning move.
I threw my dice in. Avoiding the man's gaze,
I signalled to the officer of the guard.
'Hold him'—the formal phrase—and he was gone.

It troubled me. Not that an innocent man
Should suffer crucifixion. Every year
Thousands are cross-barred here to brace an Empire:
Not all are guilty. No, it was myself
That troubled me—irresolution—
Being trapped in unwilling acts that satisfied
Neither my conscience nor the priests—wavering,
Faltering between indecisions. The third mistake.
After, for many months, ignoring Claudia,
I ruled by reason, stifling the voice that urged,
'Every denarius has a tail and head:
Can truth be absolute?'—giving an admirable
Impersonation of a man of will.

And then Mount Gerizim. A new fanatic,
This time Samaritan, was stirring followers
To search for sacred relics—Moses' or someone's,
That was the pretext—but these holy pilgrims
Took swords for digging and their secular clubs.
For once, no hesitation, I sent out
Five hundred horse and foot who scattered them

43

And gave no quarter. The Samaritans—
Those who escaped—despatched an embassy
To Vitellius, the President of Syria,
Accusing me of murder. Now I return
To face this charge before the Emperor
And find some peace again. I shall retain
My life, I think, but not my governorship.
Honourable retirement will be mine—
Space, between vineleaves in a Roman suburb,
To edit memories, to brood on error.

Now it is time. Turning toward the shore,
I nod my head, the final act of power.
The harbour wakes; at once a hundred sounds—
Men, rowlocks, ropes and chains, the first
False splash of oars. The ship moves slowly seawards.
Sudden, from shore and sea, a burst of cheering
(For me or my departure?). Above the wharves
Pile up the terraces towards the Temple;
Reflexions waver on the polished water;
The oarblades strike across it. Caesarea,
Whose beauty I had forgotten, slides away
Into the past, the unalterable past.
The harbour-opening; the bland colossi
Pivoting above us—gods and emperors,
Massive, inhuman, lifting hands to me
In a last gesture of ironic farewell.

Herod Antipas

Refers him to me for judgment?
An honour, a very great honour—
Perhaps to me, perhaps to Caesar!
Dictatorial and contemptuous he may be,
But on occasions such as this

44

He appreciates the value of tradition,
The respect due to innate kingship.
We will proceed to judgment.
Who are you?
No answer.
Overcome with awe.
Is he John the Baptist?
His beard is shorter. Cleaner, too.
No scar where the sword slit.
Another man, unless his art is great—
I have reports of his magic.
What can you do, eh? What can you show us?
Can you change stone to gold, as the crowd says?
Can you evoke lightning?
An excellent day for storms. Impressive.
Hm, sullen.
He called me a fox once.
When my agents warned him from the Tetrarchy,
'Tell that old fox,' he said. . . . I am not old.
I have my faculties, all my virility—
My women will vouch for that.
Come, show us a trick, man!
Shrink this spear to a candle-flame.
Turn your guards to jackals.
Well then, some lesser miracle—
Your dress to an imperial robe.
Still dumb. Still wordless.
It is in my mind to punish him.
Do you doubt I have power to kill you,
As I killed the Baptist?
No simpler magic, changing life to death—
A king's prerogative.
But that is precisely what Pilate wants—
Thrusting responsibility on me.
I won't oblige him.
I am a fox, eh, if not an old one.
I have great cunning and the gift of prophecy.

Return him to Caesar with my compliments.
Say I defer to him. Say I'll not presume
To sway his judgment. Say—what you will.
I'll not have him—he's a stubborn fellow.
But we must send him suitably arrayed—
If he declines to conjure it,
Provide the robe ourselves.
My old cloak—the one that warmed Judean kings—
Yes, throw it across his shoulders.
There; you shall be our embassy to Caesar:
Farewell, O King!
And grateful thanks for the royal conversation.

Mary of Bethany

M ASTER! they have taken me who have taken you;
No life is life but in your will.
It is I stand charged in the judgment hall,
Mine is the road to Caesar's hill.

No more your cool words in the heat of day,
As I crouch at your feet in forgotten sand;
No more the hours when time was a whirr of gnats,
With Heaven this courtyard, God your explaining hand.

The yard is empty—emptier than a house
That the dead have left, or an empty tomb.
A thousand years have passed, and I, the stranger,
Come to a ruined home, a wall-less room. . . .

My sister moves in her appointed way
Through constant task to common need:
To her such sacraments are real—to me
A ritual meaningless as the gentiles' creed.

O Master! they take me who have taken you;
No life is life but in your will.
It is I stand charged in the judgment hall,
Mine is the road to Caesar's hill.

Judas

You don't understand, Levi,
    Nobody understands
How the sight of his face haunts me,
    The shape of his hands.

I remember the light on his face
    When he first called me,
My mind immured from doubt
    As his hands enwalled me.

Why, in the name of his God,
    Did it have to cease?
Why sometimes that fervour returned,
    Never that peace?

I gave up more than they,
    Those net-menders;
Yet always reserved for them
    Were the throne and its splendours.

I had more faith than they.
    Not prophecies—
I'd have planted his Kingdom here
    Where God's temple is.

I'd have crowned him King in truth.—
 Roman and priest
Thrown out like a swine's offal
 When their tyranny ceased.

There was a time, I believe,
 When it might have come,
Had not Peter warped his soul
 Towards martyrdom.

Then I became the Twelfth,
 Whose silences
Were ghosts that taunted his ear
 With past uncertainties.

They only half-understood
 Where belief must lead him;
I knew he purposed his death,
 And my will denied him—

Denied him because his dying
 Meant Israel's too,
An end to dreams of dominion
 Where Jew ruled Jew.

But last week in Simon's house,
 When I protested
And he scornfully turned my rebuke
 At the ointments wasted,

His hand on the harlot's, his gaze
 Cold as his reply—
I vowed if he wished his death,
 I would help him die.

It came to me, too, that night
　　His death would sever
His hold on my life, destroy
　　That power for ever.

I was wrong. The cord, too strong,
　　Will never be broken.
I hear, behind all speech,
　　The last words spoken:

'Master, not I?'—See
　　Where he turns his head,
His eyes, his betrayed fingers
　　Tearing the bread.

God! how they twist my soul,
　　My mind is rended;
Their image imposed on my sight
　　Till life is ended.

Till life is. . . . Nor is that all.
　　I saw him to-day,
Here in the priests' court
　　When they took him away.

Calm face, still hands,
　　As if nothing moved him.
When our eyes met for the last time
　　I knew that I loved him—

I who had brought him there
　　To these indignities:
Till the sky falls and the world ends
　　My life will be his.

49

No, Levi: let me go.
I can never be free
Till I find him again in death
On another tree.

The Centurion

'WHAT is it now? More trouble?
Another Jew? I might have known it.
These Jews, they buzz around the tail of trouble
Like lascivious flies. Do they think we're here
Because we love them? Is it their climate
That holds us here? Why think, Marcellus—
By God, just dream of it. To-day in Rome,
Less than two thousand thirsty miles away,
Fountains and squares and shadowed colonnades,
Men with smooth chins and girls who sometimes wash.
Well, who is it? . . . I see.
Another to be taken to that bonehill.
They're coming now. Just listen to them!—
You'd think they had a dozen there at least.
My sword, Marcellus. I'll be back to dinner,
Unless this fellow's a reluctant dier
Who loves the world too well.

Halt! Stop that shouting. Why is he dressed like that?'
(His robes are purple. On his head
A hedge-crown. Where the thorns are driven
Berries of blood leap up. . . .) 'My orders differ.
Remove that crown—at once—return his clothes.
Kingship can wait until his throne is ready.
Till then, safe conduct. Hold your lines—
Especially that to windward: I've no fondness
For foreign spittle. Hold them. March. . . .'

'Halt! Here's the place. Set down the cross.
You three attend to it. And remember, Marcus,
The blows are struck, the nails are driven
For Roman law and Roman order,
Not for your private satisfaction.
Set to work.'
(This grass is bare, sand-coloured: the hill
Quivers with heat.) 'What? As you please.
Seamless?—Then dice for it.' (The sun
Is brutal in this land, metallic.
It works for death, not life.) 'Well, is it done?
Now nail the board above: "King of the Jews".
That turns the mockery on them. Watch them wince
At the superscription. Look, their faces!
Hate. Which man is hated most,
Myself or him? He'll serve for both:
They know their limitations. They know,
Greek, Jew or Roman, there is one command,
One only. What's his name?—
He takes it quietly. From Nazareth?
I know it well. Who would exchange it
For this sad city, and become
The food of flies? Marcus there!
Give him some wine: he won't last long.'
That strain of wrist, the arm's tension
And scarecrow hang of chest. Ah well,
Poor devil, he's got decent eyes.

John

AGONY to endure
     This living portrait of his agony—
The shifting, multicoloured mob;
Two priests in purple;

Flecks of scarlet balancing the cloak
Flung back from the Centurion's shoulder;
And above their heads, the Three
Pale against thunderous clouds. . . .
I seek for words—always my relief
As they were his. That was the bond between—
The poet in us. Others may love his words
For what they mean: I for what they are.
But now no words of mine
Are adequate. I search the Psalms—
Those Psalms of David that delighted him,
Learned in his childhood speech,
Repeated to me at night
While the others slept.
None reached, he said, the depths of spirit
David touched, nor built a surer rock
Of song to climb upon. I remember. . . .
Why art thou cast down, O my soul?
And why art thou disquieted within me?
Hope thou in God; for I shall still praise him
Who is the help of my countenance, and my God.
He hears my thoughts. Lifting his head
He wills his love towards me.
His parched lips move with mine:
All thy waves and thy billows are gone over me,
I will say unto God, my rock, Why hast thou forgotten me?
Why go I mourning because of the oppression of my enemy?
Seeing him revive and hearing 'God',
The crowd renews its mocking: 'He saved others:
Himself he cannot save!' *For thy sake*
I have borne reproach, his lips continue,
I am become a stranger unto my brethren
And an alien unto my mother's children.
For the zeal of thy house hath eaten me up,
And the reproaches of them that reproach thee
Are fallen on me. For the first time
He turns to his mother,

Mary of Nazareth, on her shelf of rock.
'Woman'—linking us with his eyes—
'Behold your son.' The voice is effort.
'Son, behold your mother.'
His lips part for a new psalm:
My God, my God, why hast thou forsaken me?—
Still in the northern form: 'Eloi! Eloi!'
None understands but I. To his enemies
He calls Elijah. To his few friends
He is drowning in despair. Only I know—
Know he controls despair
By giving shape to it, a mould of words,
Finds in undying beauty
Assurance that the spirit which gave it birth
Is also deathless. *O my God,*
I cry in the daytime and thou hearest not,
And in the night season and am not silent. . . .
A Pharisee, standing near the cross,
Has caught his words, and caps them, jeering:
He trusted in the Lord that he would deliver him,
Let him deliver him. Ignoring him,
My friend continues:
The assembly of the wicked has enclosed me.
They pierced my hands and feet,
They parted my garments among them
And cast lots upon my vesture.
Be not thou far from me, O Lord!
O my strength; haste thou to help me!
I follow him through the long Psalm
To its triumphant climax:
All the ends of the world shall remember
And turn unto the Lord.
He gazes at me for the last time,
Defeat defeated.
Then aloud, with great expense
Of power: 'It is finished.'

Yes, it is finished. Thirty years
Of godhead fleshed in words,
Words charged with God.—
Raises his head to the clouds,
Their dark violence, their threat
Of thunder. Repeats once more
From another Psalm: *Into thy hands*
O Lord, I commit my spirit.
And the head drops, jarred at the neck.
It is finished. The mob is breaking,
Thinking of shelter. Women in despair
Weeping beyond consolation.
But I, his friend,
Loving no less than they,
Feel only calm—peace
After victory. For these words
Echo in my mind and will always echo:
The ends of the world will remember
And turn to the Lord.

Mary of Nazareth—II

I FELT him under my heart, stirring:
   He was mine, mine only.
I forgot the long, divided years
   When my thoughts were lonely.

As I saw him kicking with sudden joy
   The sides of his manger,
I little thought that the God-Child there
   Was already a stranger.

I watched him grow, a sapling tree
   In a Spring meadow.
He smiled at me, and loved, and was gone
   Like a cloud's shadow.

In the temple, distracted, I knew the measure
    Of the heart's treason:
His eyes, through mine, were those of a traveller
    On some far horizon.

To his brothers' shame, he left his work
    For that homeless preaching.
He would not turn from the alien crowd
    When I was approaching.

I saw him stretched on the cross-boughed tree
    With the world mocking,
The life I carried torn with the strains
    That Death was making. . . .

Now time cannot add to my heart's sorrow.
    The years have circled.
He becomes as he was when my breasts held him,
    When a god was suckled.